Anonymous

Remarks on the New Sugar-bill and on the National

Compacts Respecting the Sugar-trade and Slave-trade

Anonymous

**Remarks on the New Sugar-bill and on the National Compacts Respecting the
Sugar-trade and Slave-trade**

ISBN/EAN: 9783337306755

Printed in Europe, USA, Canada, Australia, Japan

Cover: Foto ©ninafisch / pixelio.de

More available books at **www.hansebooks.com**

REMARKS

ON THE

NEW SUGAR-BILL,

AND ON THE

NATIONAL COMPACTS

RESPECTING THE

SUGAR-TRADE

AND

SLAVE-TRADE.

————

" Thus has the Courfe of Juftice wheel'd about."

SHAKSPEARE.

————

LONDON:

PRINTED FOR J. JOHNSON, ST. PAUL'S CHURCH-YARD,
AND J. DEBRETT, PICCADILLY.

M.DCC.XCII.

OF THE

SUGAR-BILL.

Of the Purport of the Sugar-Bill, as passed by the House of Commons, in May, 1792.

THE leading features of the bill to be discussed are these. — Whenever the average of the prices of raw (and clayed) sugar, sold in the port of London, to be taken weekly upon oath, and made public in the Gazette, exceeds, in the six weeks which respectively precede either the middle of February, June, or October, the amount of 65 s. for the hundred weight, (the duty of 15 s. thereon included,) the drawback on *raw* sugar exported to foreign parts is immediately to cease during four months, and the bounty on *refined* sugar to cease during a like term, but commencing after an interval of one month.

An exception is made as to the standard for the two periods occurring in the present year, on account of

B temporary

temporary circumſtances; the ſtandard for the firſt, which takes place in July inſtead of June, being fixed at 7 5 s. and that for the ſecond at 70 s.

The grant of licences, allowed by law to Britiſh ſhips to carry ſugars from the colonies to foreign parts,* is to be governed by the above ſtate of average-prices.

During the period that the ſuſpenſion of the draw-back or bounty takes place, particular regulations are made as to the export of ſugars to Ireland, &c.

The payment of the duties on *foreign* ſugar and coffee, while kept in certain warehouſes, is permitted to be in arrears during one year (for the accommodation of the importer).

Naſſau, with ſuch other ports of the Bahama iſlands, or of Bermuda, as ſhall be named for that purpoſe by the king in council, are made free ports for receiving foreign ſugar and coffee, under the uſual free-port regulations.

* Theſe licences are granted on condition of the ſugars being firſt brought to ſome port in Great Britain, to which place the ſhip is bound to return again within eight months after ſo touching. Sugars may be carried *directly* from the colonies to the ſouthward of Cape Finiſterre.

Remarks

Remarks on the Sugar-Bill.

In confidering this bill, it is a neceffary act of juf-tice to the Weft-India planters and merchants to pre-mife, that they have feen the late high prices of fugars with regret, though, for reafons which will be men-tioned, it was out of their power to redrefs them. They did not, indeed, at firft acknowledge the pro-priety of paffing any *law* upon the fubject, but they foon acquiefced in that propofed by adminiftration. They have no other merit than good fenfe in this pro-ceeding. They faw the rifing danger, and prudently capitulated rather than wait the ftorm in its full ex-tent; a conduct which, perhaps, deferves imitation, as well by themfelves as by government, in other concerns now under public difcuffion.

The bill in queftion may be confidered under the four views of its efficacy, its juftice, its claufes, and whether there cannot be a better bill. It is neceffary to touch upon thefe points before we go upon more interefting matter.

First, refpecting *its efficacy.*—As the colonifts and refiners each expect injury from the bill, it is difficult to fuppofe how they are each to lofe in confequence of

it;

it, and the public not to gain. — The refiners, indeed, say, that the bill will fanction high prices without infuring low ones. But it is plain that they fay this from theory only; for, when they fpeak from *experience*, they allow that the mere whifper of the bill in queftion, lowered refined goods 20s. per hundred weight, and raw fugars 10s. They fay, alfo, repeatedly, that " the export-price certainly regulates " the market ;" and it requires little difficulty to prove, that a check to exportation will, in general, accumulate a quantity of fugars in the home-market ; and that the refult of fuch accumulation will be a reduction of prices.

It admits of doubt, indeed, whether the bill may not have its object defeated from another caufe ; namely, the diminution of the cultivation of fugar, or of its confignment to the Britifh market, in confequence of the intended reftrictions. This is a fufficient reafon for not fixing the ftandard too low ; particularly as the great diftance, at which the colonift ftands removed from information, will naturally multiply his fears as to the ftate of the home-markets, where alone the law operates.

But if, after all, the bill fhall prove *inefficient*, it is natural to fuppofe that it will meet an early repeal.

But, fecondly, *is the bill juft ?*—Here we lofe fight of one of the parties interefted, namely, the colonifts ;

from

from whom all complaint is precluded by their affent
to the bill, unlefs it fhould produce unforefeen injuries
to them in its operation. — The queftion, therefore,
remains fingly with the refiners ; and, as to the refiners, the queftion reduces itfelf to this : Will the lofs,
which may occur from the bill, fall upon *raw* or upon
refined fugars ?

We may anfwer as follows.—The colonift is bound
fafter to his eftate than the refiner to his trade ; his culture cannot change its object without great lofs ; and,
fince each year's crop is in cultivation fixteen or eighteen
months before it arrives at market, he is pledged to
fubmit to whatever prices a diftant futurity fhall produce for him with refpect to the fugars he fends
here ; and, as he knows little befides what appears
in his own ifland, his difadvantages in this refpect become increafed. In any event the colonift muft fuffer long before he abandons lightly ; he muft fuffer
long before the public will commiferate him, while
monopoly and extortion are the ready watch-words to
bear him down.—The cafe is every way the reverfe
for the refiner. His forefight is called for refpecting
fhort periods ; he fees, at one view, the produce of
all colonies and the demands of *all* nations ; he can foon
retrench or quit his concerns ; if he buys high and fells
low at one time, he may reverfe it at another ; if hurt,
he has the public fympathy on his fide, and is fure of
a repeal of the law aggrieving him ; and, by keeping
his

his article, which he may do for four months with
little lofs, the foreign market may again open to him.
Even the fufpenfion of his operations, if it fhould become ferious, being a grievance common to all in his
trade, muft receive compenfation generally, or the
profeffion would be relinquifhed.

There can be little doubt, therefore, either that the
lofs which occurs will fall on the colonift, fince the pro-
ducer *muft* fell and the refiner *need* not buy ; or elfe that
any injury received by the refiner will be a full motive
for altering the law.

Thirdly, we are to fpeak of the *claufes of the bill.*

And here we may obferve, firft, that a fpace of
time *intervenes* before the law acts upon *refined* fugars;
and, as refined fugars are all that have hitherto been
exported to foreigners, they are all in which the refiner
has any concern. This provifion then enables the refiner
to get rid of large quantities of his goods; and as, by
the very nature of the law, the goods muft have been
bought cheap and fold dear, (that is, bought under
the average and fold at or above it,) he can have little
to complain of; fince there is no period of the year at
which the refiners cannot, in one month, fupply more
than is ufually required for four months foreign trade;
and fpeculators will always offer to purchafe this fupply,
fhould not foreigners do it in the firft inftance.

As

As to the clause creating high rates for the standards for the two *first periods* named in the bill, we have only to obferve that they are temporary; and were fuggefted partly to protect the fugar refiners themfelves, who fay that their fuite of refinery-proceffes laft for five or fix months before they are intirely clofed (though fome of their refined goods are produced from them within the firft fix weeks). They were alfo partly intended to relieve perfons who have purchafed fugars in the colonies at the great prices, induced by the late prices in Europe: fugars, which are not yet all brought to Europe; and which, if fold even at the prefent rates, will occafion a lofs of 25 per cent. Befides, as the adoption of this fugar-bill, by the parliament of Ireland, will only happen, by virtue of the arrangement made between the two countries, in four months after its meeting next winter; an earlier reduction of the ftandard would not only be nugatory, from the impoffibility of putting a check to exportation to foreign parts through the medium of Ireland; but would contribute to confirm the rivalfhip of the Irifh refiners.

The rate for the *permanent* ftandard admits of feveral obfervations. — Firft, the buyer, in order to place himfelf out of the reach of danger, will purchafe fugars at prices fo low, as amply to allow for the interference of it; and, as the feller will precipitate his fale from correfponding prepoffeffions, the fear produced by the ftandard will operate *both* upon buyer and feller.

Hence

Hence the standard of the bill will virtually become nominal, and another *effective* standard be created, several shillings below it. — A second observation on the permanent standard is, that, though it is formed from averages, it is itself a *ne plus ultra*; and, though derived from a medium, it fixes a *maximum*. This point of excess is deemed to exist whenever the average-price of raw and clayed sugars of all qualities stands at 65*s.* When this occurs, the average of the foreign market must be 25 per cent. higher than this excess, in order to admit of sugar being sent there loaded with the British duties and accompanied with the various charges of conveyance. — The permanent standard admits of another remark with reference to the colonist. Having no bounty at low prices, its operation, as far as it is favourable, is his sole compensation when distressed by low prices. It stands as his farthest hope, his *ultima Thule*, in a case where his inclination was before unlimited. It has already been observed, that a deduction is to be made for so much of the standard only as is nominal; and that clayed sugars, being employed to inflame the average, the standard will operate by anticipation. — In the result, then, it will be found, that the standard does not allow, in any case, a receipt of 40 per cent. surplus beyond the planter's *living profit*; a fluctuation much exceeded by that in articles of British agriculture, and far short of
the

the proportion of depreciation which fugars have often experienced.

Fourthly, another topic remains refpecting the bill. *Is this the beft law that can be?* — It will be proper to anfwer this query fully when we hear better laws propofed.

The beft meafure would be *no law*; and the next beft would be to have the law as *temporary* as the occafion for it. But, as the law is defigned to obviate public uneafinefs and to reduce prices, which all parties have allowed to have been exceffive, and as it is hoped that it will fucceed in both objects, no oppofition is offered to it by the colonifts.

But it is proper to notice that this bill is only partially formed upon the model of the *corn-trade fyftem.* The corn-trade laws are defigned to equalize the prices of corn, through a courfe of years, by checking exportation at high prices, and giving a bounty on exportation in cafe of low ones: they are defigned to reduce prices by encouraging production; and they operate upon a commodity which is fubject to little or no manufacture. Not fo this bill; which is primarily defigned rather to *reduce* prices, than either to equalize them or to multiply production; for, it checks high prices, and gives no bounty in the cafe of low ones; and, as none but refined fugars ufually go abroad, it renders the refiner at all times a timid purchafer, even where he purchafes at all, left he fhould be furprifed in the midft of the procefs, neceffary to fit his commodity for the foreign market.

As to the propofal for an immediate fufpenfion of the drawback and bounty, it is founded upon natural, but by no means upon politic, notions. Upon many fubjects there are what may be called *firft fuggeftions*; but, where thefe fuggeftions are not adopted in common practice, it is natural to prefume that they are objectionable. The firft idea for procuring cheap prices is to ufe conftraint, which often fucceeds for the exifting quantities of any article. But the power of the legiflator goes no farther: he cannot conftrain the *wills* of men: he may as well, in Mr. Locke's phrafe, hedge in the cuckoo. The colonifts, therefore, will not continue to furnifh frefh fupplies of fugar, if they are not paid, for what they have before brought, to their full fatisfaction. The inftances of the fhort-lived triumph of conftraint are fo many, that it is now the tritest of all maxims in political economy, that plenty is to be produced by liberty and encouragement inftead of force.

So much for the bill, the merit of all of whofe claufes it is by no means requifite to difcufs. The queftion is about its fyftem; avowedly a fyftem of experiment; and not volunteered by government, but produced in deference to the public alarm.

It

If any doubts are left about the prudence of the bill, they respect, first, what has been so often alluded to, the operation it may have upon importation from the colonies; and, next, the possibility that the vague fears or hopes of re-exporters may cause greater shipments to foreign markets than would happen without the bill.

Various miscellaneous topics remain, and these will be ranged under two heads; namely, the objections urged by refiners; and the objections urged in debate in the House of Commons.

Objections of the Refiners.

I. The refiners say that the colonists can *command* prices.

To the answer already given on this subject, we may add, that, in great commodities, prices are commanded by the will neither of buyer nor seller. The great regulators of markets are *quantity and demand*. Even in the case of the East-India company, which, in many respects, acts as one man, competition, though operating only on one side, produces the greatest ef-

fects;

fects; but in the West-India trade, it operates on both sides. — The sugar-trade is a monopoly as to the *whole* of it; but it retains competition and jealousy as to its *parts*. — The sugar-refiner, who was questioned as an evidence upon the subject before the House of Commons, confessed, that he neither knew nor had ever heard of any combination of West-India merchants, respecting sugar. So vast an object as sugar, amounting to several millions annually, placed in various hands variously circumstanced, is not susceptible of combination. It admits of speculation, but not of combination; it admits of prudence, but not of concert. The resource of the merchant is simply to *fell with judgment*; and perhaps the best judgment dictates that which exactly favours, or at least does not counteract, that most desirable object, a gradual consumption of the annual crop; namely, to hasten the early sales of the season, and to protract the late ones, and to be always selling something when there is a large stock on hand, since a large stock cannot be disposed of in a moment. If the merchant has any other rule, whether general or occasional, it requires secrecy rather than combination; because it is the interest of each merchant to outdo his neighbour. In general, the merchants seldom keep their sugar long, either because of the loss in keeping, arising from the waste of the commodity in its raw state, together with its various attendant charges; or because some of

them

them are needy, others of them diſlike trouble, and others act thus from ſyſtem. — The only moment, when the Weſt-India merchants can pretend to have any influence upon the market, is very early or very late in the annual ſeaſon; but as this happens, by the very ſuppoſition, when the market is moſt defective in its ſupply, and as it is generally agreed, among conſiderate political writers, that nothing better effects an even diſtribution of a commodity, (and, as we ſhall ſoon have reaſon to add, gives it a more equal and reaſonable price,) than the gradual ſale of it, this influence is to be deemed a benefit, rather than otherwiſe. If the merchant, on theſe occaſions, ſhould unfortunately ſell precipitately, a middle party occurs, namely, the grocers and refiners, who would take care to put the public under contribution for any natural price, which the merchants had omitted to obtain. — And we may here obſerve, by the by, that the provident refiners have no objection to an advance of the prices of raw ſugars at the *end* of the annual ſeaſon, after they have finiſhed their own purchaſes, and have only to conſider their ſales.

II. Reſpecting the ſuppoſed wilfulneſs of the conduct of the coloniſts, as to the late exceſſive prices of ſugar (without which wilfulneſs that exceſs cannot be imputed to them as cenſurable); the charge is eaſily done away, not only by the remarks made as to the immutability

inimutability of great markets, but by the following
confiderations.

In the laft winter the more difcreet colonifts would
have reduced the prices of fugar confiderably, had it
been in their power ; as producing merely a temporary
benefit, and tending to eftablifh the evil of permanent
reftrictions. But, firft, no man could rule his neighbour, and fuch a meafure on the part of individuals
only, would have been futile and ridiculous ; next, if
the colonifts had fold low to the refiners and grocers,
yet, fince thefe would have got the utmoft poffible price
afterwards from the public, they would have loft their
own profit, without obtaining credit with any one for
moderation ; and, laftly, they had, in general, fuffered heavily by paft calamities, and anticipated future ones of a ftill heavier nature from the temper of
the public. Nor is it to be forgotten, that whatever
were the prices paid, a part of them· were repaid by
foreigners, and the reft only formed a transfer of property between fubject and fubject.

III. But, fay the refiners, the planters gained
£ 2,657,768 upon the importation of laft year, compared, quantity for quantity, with the importations
between 1770 and 1776. — This ftatement is capable
of very fatisfactory explanations.

For example, inftead of the quantity brought for
home confumption, it fpeaks of the total importation, and confequently is liable to the remark juft
made,

made, that the price of fo much of the quantity as is re-exported to foreigners turns to national profit. Again, whatever be the inconvenience from the price fuffered by the public, it was, as has been ftated, in a manner *involuntary* on the fide of the planters. By the prefent bill, alfo, it is propofed, that this inconvenience, to whatever caufe it may have been owing, fhall not, under the fame circumftances, ever again return; fince future prices are permanently limited, by this bill, to an amount far lower than thofe already obtained. The refiners, likewife, have allowed, upon another occafion, that quality of raw fugars has, of late years, been very confiderably improved; which improvement, being the refult both of care and expence in the colonifts, fairly merits compenfation on the part of the purchafer.

But this is not all. The particular expences attending Weft-India Eftates have lately heavily been increafed, in confequence of the check given (folely for the accommodation of Great Britain) to the intercourfe with North America; a check which has raifed the price of feveral extenfive objects of purchafe, and lowered that of feveral extenfive objects of fale; and thefe expences have increafed alfo in confequence of the increafed value of negroes, and of the fuperior expenditure now laudably ufed in providing for them. Cafualties, to an immenfe amount, might likewife find their enumeration in this place; but thefe will be touched

upon

upon hereafter, especially as they do not all of them make part of the permanent charges attendant upon West-India Estates; though it might be expected, that, when considered as casualties, they would at least operate in allaying the ill-judged resentment in the public, if not in exciting its commiseration. — But there is another head of expences, the justice of which it is impossible not to admit, and of the weight of which all men are made sensible by their personal experience; namely, that general one which is consequent upon the operation of public taxes. It is a known axiom in politics that taxes ultimately distribute themselves so equally upon the public as eventually to raise the prices of all commodities; each man repaying himself, for taxes which he pays on other articles, by advancing the price of his own; and it would be hard indeed, if, while others *receive* more to pay with, they should refuse to reimburse those who are equally sufferers by this re-action and interchange of the public burthens.

The most important observation, however, on this head still remains to be noticed at some length. — It is this. The price of sugars at the highest period was compared by the refiners with that of the lowest; and this was so low, owing to abundant crops in our own and the neighbouring islands, as to bring the planters into debt. — But, to give force to this consideration, a great commercial axiom is to be mentioned, which

is,

is, that quantity and price are not *correlative* and cor-
respording in years of high and low prices. For high
years, hear Mr. King, as quoted by Dr. Davenant.
" *One*-tenth of defect in the harvest will raise the price
" of corn about three-tenths above the common rate ;
" *two*-tenths of defect will raise the price eight-tenths ;
" and *three*-tenths deficiency will advance it about one
" and six tenths or sixteen-tenths." Hence we see,
that, when quantity goes decreasing in an arithme-
tical ratio, price goes on rapidly increasing in more
than a geometrical ratio.—In short, when the commodity is scarce, the *commodity* is, as it were, *put to
auction*; but, when it is plentiful, it is the money
which is put to auction; and, at this auction, not
only fears and rivalships influence, but men measure
value by the degree of their own desires compared with what they can afford ; whereas, in the
usual course of things, prices obtain a proportion determined by the usual rates of costs and of profits upon
what is sold.—But these distorted prices naturally occur in a still greater degree in cases of *scarcity* than of
plenty; for, as most persons contract their demands
for expensive articles upon an increase of price, so
most especially do the poor for articles consumed by
them, particularly when they are not articles of prime
necessity; or, in other words, price *falls more* with
plenty than it rises with scarcity.—We may add, that,
as a series of scanty years brings on a *habit* of high prices,

D fo

fo the reverfe happens in a feries of plentiful years; and, in like manner, as a crop, bought under a continued *apprehenfion of fcarcity* naturally acquires exaggerated prices, fo does a crop, bought under oppofite perfuafions, experience proportionally lower prices. Thefe circumftances have each refpectively operated upon the two periods of fales brought under comparifon by the refiners. — We may therefore conclude this head by obferving, that, the price in each *period* having fo much differed from its natural level, a *double* caufe arifes to widen their *mutual divergence.**

The remaining replies to the refiners will be more briefly difcuffed.—Let us proceed, then,

IV. To detect a confiderable miftake in their conclufions, drawn from the fuppofed average-prices of fugar in Jamaica. — Here we may obferve, that they have wholly overlooked that Jamaica fugars are fold, not as in this country by the long hundred weight of 112 lbs, but by the fhort or futtle hundred weight of 100 lbs, which makes a difference of $\frac{1}{7}$ in their eftimate. — Next, they forget a wafte in tranfporting the commodity from the Weft-Indies to Great Britain equal to another $\frac{1}{9}$. The cafk or package alfo cofts eleven fhillings, which is not included in the coft of the commodity, which makes eight-pence addition to each hundred weight; and the ifland-commiffion and other

---

* It follows, from what is faid above, that a large crop may fell for lefs than a fmall one ; and *vice verfâ.*

charges

charges amount to one shilling more. These mistakes, added together, would make a difference of 6 s. or 7 s. in each hundred weight; but from this, however, some deduction is to be made, on account of the island-markets for sugar (for reasons not worth mentioning) being usually found above their true rate.—The living price, therefore, necessary for the planter, according to these data, (for the accuracy of which the colonists are not responsible,) turn out 51 s. instead of 46 s. per hundred weight in this market; which does not vary much from that actually obtained from 1784 to 1790. (See the latter report of the sugar refiners page 11, there being errors in their calculation at page 33.)

V. A still greater misstatement, than that which precedes, respects what the refiners say about the price of sugar at Bourdeaux, in October last. — The paper-money, or assignats, of France, when first issued, lost only when contrasted with gold and silver; but, when other articles were bought up to send to foreign markets, all exportable commodities rose suddenly and rapidly (leaving other articles much as before). Previous to this moment, the rate of exchange certainly admitted cheap purchases, since sugar, which cost 37 s. per hundred weight, would have cost 56 s. at the par of exchange. — Things are now altered; and our sugars are not only nominally cheaper, but the intrinsic difference between them is increased,

owing

owing to our raw fugars, compared with theirs, being avowedly of fuperior quality.

VI. The refiners are guilty of another mifreprefen-tation, when they fay, that no events in the French colonies operated on the Britifh market, till the great revolt at St. Domingo ;* whereas it is notorious, that Martinique remained torn in pieces by diffentions du-ring two years; and that neither Guadaloup nor To-bago have been wanting in their difcords or diftreffes. Foreigners, who faw all thefe things cooly, as by-ftanders, feared that fome great calamity to cultiva--

---

* Having fpoken of St. Domingo and its diftreffes, it will be al-lowable to relate an incident honourable to our countrymen, and which, therefore, cannot be made too public.

The firft authentic news of the St. Domingo revolt was received in England, and thence communicated, by exprefs, to the houfe of Meffrs. Collow, Carmichael, and Co. at Havre de Grace, in France. —— Thefe gentlemen, inftead of ufing the intelligence to their own profit in that and other French ports, by buying up fecretly Weft-India produce, in order to avail themfelves of its approaching rife ; went directly to the municipality, made public their information, and got couriers difpatched to the other ports and to the National Affembly at Paris, in order to put every feller in France on a par with the buyer. The defign fucceeded, and, on the pittance of colonial produce then remaining in the hands of the firft importers, which was thus enhanced in value, perfons in-terefted in the French colonies, have for a time been enabled to fup-port themfelves. The French were grateful, the Britifh name was honoured, and the parties, it is believed, do not to this moment re-pent the generous conduct they purfued.

tion woul' be the refult; and *their fears* foon raifed fugars in the European markets.

In extenuation for the refiners, it muft here be al lowed, that they do not pretend to know much beyond their own country and trade; — otherwife it muft have been expected from them, in candour, to have ftated, that prices have long been rifing, not only from various caufes which have before been mentioned, but from drought, hurricanes, war, and an infect called the *borer*, which, though now on the decline, had lately fuddenly infefted moft of the Leeward iflands, and has injured the Britifh empire in particular, for feveral years, to the amount of more than half a million fterling per annum. In fhort, the European market has never once, if we may ufe that expreffion, been thoroughly faturated with fugar fince the American war. But, happily, the Englifh iflands are now doing their part handfomely, if they are allowed to do it *freely*; the caufes of fcarcity being rapidly difappearing, and their cultivation having evidently greatly advanced, fince, in fpite of *every difafter*, the quantity imported is allowed to be augmented fince the American war; and therefore, without difafters, the quantity would have been greatly increafed.

VII. This leads to another confideration.—It is faid by the refiners or their friends, that it is the nature of our fugar-colonies to be fubject to *extreme uncertainties* in their crops.

Refpecting,

Refpecting, however, the prefent deficiency of fugar in Europe, (I fay in Europe, for, Great Britain
has received as well its ufual fupply for home-con-
fumption, as its ufual furplus for re-exportation,) let
it not be attributed to the Britifh planter, fince it is
folely owing to the calamities of the French iflands;
calamities which have by no means originated from
the accidents of nature, but from political revolutions,
external and internal. Befides, whatever is the evil,
the bill profeffes to undertake its cure, as far as refpects Great Britain. — As to natural evils in general,
they are not more prevalent in our fugar-colories,
than in other countries within the tropics. Nature
acts there on a larger and more gigantic fcale. Their
rain, their thunder, their ftorms, their infects, are all
remarkable in their ufual appearances; and, when
they rife beyond their common level, they are truly
extraordinary. But this ought not to excite any new
alarms. The fugar-iflands are our old acquaintance:
we have before us their hiftory for more than a century and a half; we know their beft and their worft;
and that cafualties in them can only be temporary. —
If we think that the Eaft Indies are freer than the Weft
from natural difafters, remember the celebrated famine of Bengal, and look at the late accounts from
Lord Cornwailis and other quarters of India. Obferve, too, our farmers in Great Britain, who, notwithftanding the varieties of their culture, which render

 der a total failure of all their crops peculiarly difficult, yet are affailed by a thoufand viciffitudes; moft of which, however, as they leave their landlords untouched, becaufe depending upon fixed rents, permit our landed gentlemen to remain ignorant of the fluctuations belonging to their own climate and fituation.

VIII. But, fay the refiners, our refining-trade is decreafed. — This is readily allowed; but the confumption of *fugar in general* has increafed: for, it is confumed raw inftead of refined. But this is an explanation of the nature of the objection, rather than a full removal of its amount. It muft, therefore, be confeffed, that, by the check given to the refinery, in confequence of the high prices of raw fugar, the public fuffers in its gratifications, and the refiner in his trade. — But the anfwer, fo often reforted to, again occurs: — the bill endeavours to remedy the evil, and the coloniits affent to the mode employed by it for the purpofe.

IX. In a remaining particular, we have to complain, it is to be hoped, rather of the want of caution, than of the ill-intention, of the refiners; for it is certainly, in part, owing to their ftatements, that the public conceive that a confiderable bounty ftill exifts upon the export of refined fugars.

There are both a fact and an explanation to ftate in reply on this fubject. — The *fact*, alluded to, is, that
the

the total annual a nt of the bounty, according to
the fhewing of fugar refiners themfelves, is only
about £ 8000 p. annum; which, to a tax amounting
to a million per annum, bears the proportion of abouc
⅟ per cent. a proportion which cannot in any view or
to any per! appear confiderable.* The colonifts,

* It is fingular that the refiners have never given a comparative
ftate of the duty on raw fugar and the bounty (fo called) on refined
sugar as it now ftands. Was this with the liberal view of leaving the
public impreffed with the idea, that the colonifts ftill enjoyed the
full benefit of the *late* furplus bounty, upon which fo much has been
defcanted? Such ftratagems, if intended, are always fhort lived.

The matter really ftands thus, upon their own data compared with
the ftatute-book. Out of a ton of raw fugar the refiners allow that
they make nine cwt. of loaf and lump fugar, and five cwt. of baftard;
but, by law, the drawback or bounty on the firft article, at 26 s. per
cwt. is £ 11 . 14; and, upon the latter, at 15 s. per cwt. is £ 3 . 15;
making together £ 15 . 9. Deduct from this £ 15, the prefent duty
on a ton of raw fugar, and there remains only a bounty of 9 s. even
upon *this* calculation, for fo much refined fugar (namely, 14 cwt.) as
correfponds to a ton, or 20 cwt. of raw fugar.—This proportion, upon
the total average-export of refined fugar for nine years, (reckoning
from 1783 to 1791, each inclufive,) gives about £ 8000, as above
ftated, for the total furplus of bounty; being in the proportion of about
⅟ per cent. upon the fum-total of balance of the prefent annual fugar-
tax after deducting drawbacks and bounties; and about $\frac{1}{11}$ part of
the total of the bounty, as it is called; which bounty, it may
be perceived, deferves no other general name than that of a fim-
ple drawback.—The laft of the comparative ftatements on this fubject, *exhibited by the refiners*, makes a lofs of £ 2 . 6 . 8 to the re-
venue, inftead of 9 s. as , forming a difference of more than
fix to one.

however,

however, who have no other data to found themselves upon, than the reports of the fugar refiners, which are little to be praifed for their impartiality, doubt even the exiſtence of the difference. But fuffice it to fay, that Mr. Pitt, who held the fcales between the contending parties with an even hand, and who watched the turn with an eagle's eyes, will fcarcely vary from the account here given.—So much for the *fact*.

Now for the *explanation* promifed. — The ſtatutebook applies the word DRAWBACK to the tax repaid upon the exportation of *raw* fugar, and the word BOUNTY to the money paid upon the exportation of what is *refined*. The word drawback accurately expreffes its meaning; for, (excepting the gain to government, by intereſt, in confequence of having had a depofit of the tax for fome time in its hands, and excepting the duty retained on the quantity wafted and plundered, while the fugar continued in a Britiſh port,) the original duty, paid at importation, is refunded on exportation, without diminution or addition. — But the cafe was *once* different as to the bounty. Government, to encourage the refinery-trade, gave a bounty on refined fugar, in addition to the drawback due upon it; and, in this ſtate, both amounts obtained the *collective name* of bounty. The memory of this fituation of things ſtill continues its influence in preferving to the drawback on refined fugars the name of *bounty*; though, in effect, it is now become nearly

E   an

an exact *compenfation* for the duty paid on the extra quantity of raw fugars *expended* in producing a given quantity of refined. — Thus it happens in trade as in politics, that names are often retained, when the inftitutions to which they are applied have wholly changed their nature.

Thus far what has been faid, refpecting the refiners, has been merely *defenfive* in the behalf of the colonies. But, the ftatements of the refiners having gone far with the public in contributing to excite prejudices, it is neceffary, by a few words, to reduce thefe ftatements to their true value. For this purpofe, only two remarks, in the way of criticifms, will be neceffary upon their conduct.

The firft is, that the late high prices of refined fugar are in part to be afcribed to the fugar refiners themfelves; which is proved as follows. — The difference of the value of the *average* of raw fugars, compared with that of low lump fugar, (which is the leaft variable of the feveral fpecies of refined fugars,) was in fact, for the years 1788, 1789, and 1790, taking one year with another, found to be about 17 s. per hundred weight. — One of the refiners who was examined before the Houfe of Commons, intimated, indeed, that the amount of this difference was much more than either 15 s. or 20 s. and certainly the higher is the price of the raw commodity, the greater does the difference

between

between the two articles become, (on account of the increafe of lofs upon fo much raw fugar as is wafted in its converfion into refined.*) But, after every allowance of this kind, it is impoffible to conceive that the difference has ever, for example, reached 26 s. But it was admitted in evidence, that, during the laft winter, this difference was carried, by the refiners, up to 36 s. and when the " whifper of the bill" afterwards operated, while raw fugars only admitted a fall of 10 s. per hundred weight, low lump fugar became reduced 20 s.—In fhort, as the refiners alone were provided with the article which was in requeft with foreigners, and as delay was requifite for the procefs by which its quantity was to be increafed, they profited, like other traders, by the exigency of circumftances. — In this, no one can blame them for any thing but inconfiftency, and for reproaching others for what they have done themfelves; fince nothing can be more reafonable than that traders fhould take advantage of occafional gains, to compenfate for occafional loffes.

But, to proceed to the fecond propofed criticifm on the conduct of the refiners. — Their new zeal, like that of the other profelytes, is at prefent apparently ar-

* It is to be obferved, that, during thefe years and until laft Chriftmas, there has generally been a rifing market; confequently, the refiners profited conftantly by the rife of fugars in the interval between their purchafe of the raw fugar, to the moment of felling it in its refined ftate; amounting upon an average to feveral months.

dent

dent for the public; but we are not therefore to give
the.n credit for entire fincerity, when we find that they
have made common caufe with the colonifts for near
fixty years, in obtaining what *they* ftate to be an improper bounty upon the exportation of refined fugars
(of which defcription the whole export of fugar to foreign parts had long confifted). It is notorious, that
the colonifts were wholly ignorant of the real amount of
this bounty;* but not fo the refiners. The fact was
known to each and to all of them; and, while they be-
nefited by it, the meafure was right and was political.
--But the fcene has lately changed, and, with it, their
opinion. When the price of refined fugars rofe, fo as..
to affect its confumption in the home (which is its moft.
confiderable) market, and when their capital became
fo loft in the high price of raw fugars, that it would not.
enable them to go through the fame quantity of *work*,..
upon which alone their gains depended; then, and
very naturally, they founded an alarm. But they did..
it, methinks, a little unhandfomely; fince a portion
either of good fellowfhip, of modefty, or charity,
might have induced them to have omitted the oppro-
brious terms of exactors and monopolifts, which they
now apply without ceremony to their old companions.

* The Weft-India meeting was, by a miftake, led into a belief,
that the difference between the average-price of raw fugars and low
lump fugars was 40 s. and made a propofition to adminiftration, founded upon this error, which was afterwards retracted on their part.

—It

— It is neceffary, however, to do the refiners the juftice to fay, that the new politics of fome of their body
are not fatisfactory to all of them ; for, there are fome
who perceive, that, however the drawing back of the
tax on fugars, which are refined, may, for the moment, prejudice them, yet that permanently, and where
prices are not exceffive, the principle of it is both juft
to the colonifts and beneficial to themfelves and to
their country. No one will wonder therefore, if, upon
a change of fituation, thofe very refiners, who are now
moft clamarous for an abolition of what is called the
bounty and the drawback, fhould be found petitioning
to have an increafe of the bounty to an amount more
fuitable to the meaning of that term.

So much for the refiners. — We now proceed to
another and more dignified body ; the antagonifts of
the colonifts in the Houfe of Commons, who have
made fome few remarks in addition to thofe previoufly
fuggefted by the refiners.

Replies to fome Remarks made in the Houfe of Commons.

I. One member intimated, that all the fugar produced in the world does not equal all the demand. —
But demand does not mean a mere wifh to *confume*,
but

but an ability also to compensate to the cultivator for his expences, combined with that wish. — The law of Providence is *nil sine labore*; and that the actual supply has been at least equal to this sort of demand, we may conclude both from our always having had a surplus of British sugar to export to foreign nations, and from immense means of increasing the general supply of European nations existing in our own and foreign colonies, which have not yet been called into action.

II. The same gentleman stated that foreigners would (as he believed) take our surplus sugars though burthened with more or less of the British tax remaining from its original importation. — But, if foreigners will purchase our sugars in spite of a tax annexed, the complaints of the refiners, that they shall suffer by a bill which occasionally prohibits the drawing back of the tax, cannot altogether be well founded.

III. Another remark, from the same quarter, (which in every view is one highly respectable,) was, that every shilling in the standard fixed by the bill produces a difference of £75,000 without the duty, and £90,000 including it, in the value of the sugars imported annually. — But, admitting the assertion to be in itself correct, what conclusion is to be drawn from it? Does not the question still remain, whether this shilling in the standard is rightly placed or not; a large sum like this being as heavy for one side to *lose*

as

as it is for the other fide to pay; and, indeed, more
fo, fince the *whole property* of the fugar-planter is at-
tached to the price of his produce, while only a very
fmall part of that of the confumer is interefted in it?
In fhort, it feems improper to meafure this queftion
in the way of amounts; the only queftion as to the
ftandard being, *What is equitable?*

IV. A fecond member affirmed pofitively, that
the new law would raife the prices of fugar. — But this
is to fuppofe a perverfe public and little wifdom
in the framers of the bill; and, as was very per-
tinently replied, it is fcarcely verified by the experience exhibited under the corn-bill. Is it becaufe
fugar by being kept at home is rendered plentiful, that its price is to increafe? — But as this objection has been already fully confidered; we fhall only
remark, that for all fugar arriving in Great Britain,
the prices, under the bill, *may* become lower, but
(unlefs by a new increafe of the export of refined fugar) they *cannot become higher*.

V. A third gentleman obferved, that the value of
the *whole* exports to the Weft Indies is not equal to
the difference of profit which fell laft year to the fhare
of the colonifts. — But, without entering here into the
chain of arguments connected with this topic, it feems
fufficient to remark, that the colonifts, with little or
no exception, refide either here or in the iflands; and
that what of their profits is not exported, or kept to

be

be fpent at home, is faved (as happens with other furplus incomes) to accumulate new wealth for Britifh ufes.

VI. Several of the fpeakers feemed by no means aware of the ufes of exportation. *Enough*, however, according to the adage, *is enough, and a little to fpare.* It is hard to keep a refervoir always replenifhed, which is always in a ftate of fluctuation, without a conftant ftream runs through it, to make irregularities difap-pear. Exportation gives this ftream. If we pufh the colonies too hard, they will abandon a part of our fup-ply.*

Various other objections were treated in the courfe of the debate; but, as they have been noticed in

* " As the Britifh confumers receive their fhare in the benefits
" rendered by the monopoly-fyftem to the navigation, merchants,
" and refiners, of Great Britain, they can in juftice claim no more
" than a right of pre-emption with regard to fugar; and ought to
" fuffer the furplus, beyond their confumption, to go to foreign
" markets, without adding new burthens to thofe already impofed
" by a circuitous voyage and various mercantile profits in favour
" of the mother-country, which renders the article much dearer,
" at the fame nominal price, to foreigners than to themfelves. The
" foreigner, independent of the expence of tranfporting the com-
" modity to the place of his refidence, buys nothing for which a
" Britifh fubject choofes to pay an equal price; which the body
" of Britifh confumers are known to be better able to pay than any
" other."— *Weft-India Memorial to Miniftry, February* 28, 1792.

the

the anfwers made to the refiners, and will be farther
noticed in the fecond part of this pamphlet, we fhall
haften to give a moft brilliant paffage from a fpeech
made by Mr. Fox, in a debate during the American
war, refpecting the admiffion of prize-fugars to home-
confumption, as taken from the printed accounts of it.

‘ Mr. *Fox* fpoke ably on the fame fide. * * * * “ The
“ oppreffive confequences of the war on our Weft-
“ India plantations (he faid) were more intolerable than
“ could be defcribed. Befides all the loffes they fuftain-
“ ed, the price of fhipping and infurance was enor-
“ moufly increafed, and the expence of their home-
“ defence was greater in proportion than that of Great
“ Britain. The ifland of Jamaica alone expended annu-
“ ally £ 160,000 though her eftablifhment before the
“ war was only £ 60,000. What then was to be the
“ equivalent for fuch burthens? how were they to
“ ftruggle againft all the calamities of war, but by ta-
“ king advantage of any cafual high price which their
“ commodities might bear in our market? But, in-
“ ftead of this, *new innovations* were now attempted,
“ by which every profpect of fupport would be defea-
“ ted in future; and this on no other plan but a tempo-
“ rary fcarcity of fugar, which the events of war
“ alone had produced. Our convoy laft year had
“ been taken; and, in confequence of that, there could
“ not be found fhipping to tranfport the growth of
“ our iflands; but it was univerfally admitted, that the

F   “ crop

" crop now on hand exceeded every thing that had
" been remembered; and, in a fhort time, a fleet
" was expected with an ample fupply for our mar-
" kets.

" The noble lord had called the non-importation of
" prize-fugars a mere cuftom-houfe regulation, and
" therefore thought the rule might eafily be difpenfed
" with; but he muft inform his lordfhip, that a com-
" pact *more folemn than any act of parliament could create*,
" made that rule not to be infringed; for we had
" monopolifed the produce of our plantations, by
" unnatural reftrictions on their trade. This was the
" only country in Europe in which they were permitted
" by our laws to fell their crops; furely then, by every
" principle of reafon and natural juftice, they fhould
" alfo have an exclufive accefs to our markets, a mo-
" nopoly fubfifting on one fide, neceffarily implying
" a monopoly alfo on the other. There was not
" any written agreement, but there was *fomething more*
" *fubftantial*; there was monopoly againft monopoly.
" The Weft-India planters were confined in the fale of
" their commodities to Britain, and Britain was confi-
" ned to take thofe commodities from them, and them
" only. This tacit bargain was confirmed not by
" words but by deeds. The planters enjoyed certain
" privileges, and for thofe privileges they gave fome-
" thing in return, an *ample equivalent*; fo that there
" was *quid pro quo*, which was allowed in the civil law,

" to

" to be a formal ratification of any compact or bar-
" gain;—but, as it would feem, parliament were *eager*
" *to feize*, but not ready to grant, the advantages of a
" reciprocal monopoly. When any thing is to be
" gained, ' we have a monopoly of your trade;'. but
" when any thing is to be loft, and it is faid, ' we plan-
" ters have a monopoly of your cuftoms,' it is replied,
" we have a fupreme jurifdiction over you, and are
" bound by no tacit or implied contracts.—According
" to this doctrine, (continued Mr. Fox,) the Weft-
" India planters need never read a newfpaper or ga-
" zette; there is no room for the indulgence of curi-
" ofity. If any profperous event happens, as the
" taking of a fugar-ifland, their lofs is evident; fince
" thereby the value of the growth of their plantations
" is diminifhed. If, on the contrary, an adverfe ac-
" cident takes place, and that any of our iflands
" be taken, the planter fhares with others in the
" lofs. * * * *

" He obferved, that if our *manufactory* was decay-
" ing, from the lofs of our iflands, and confequent
" want of commodity, to allow the importation of
" prize-fugars could at beft only be a temporary and
" precarious remedy: at the conclufion of the war,
" fuch a refource muft neceffarily fail; and, in the
" mean time, plunder was not an eligible bafis of
" trade. He admitted, indeed, that the fugar-ma-
" nufacture in this country was going to decay;

" the

" the reafon was natural, we were lofing our fugar-
" iflands. But we were not to reftore that ma-
" nufacture by ruining the planters; who *prefuming*
" *upon the monopoly*, had laid out their fortunes in
" fugar-plantations, and who confequently muft be
" ruined if they cannot get as extenfive a market
" for their commodity as their plantations and ex-
" pences require.

" In the courfe of his fpeech he obferved fome
" geftures of Lord North, from which he pre-
" dicted that he fhould have the honour of agree-
" ing with his lordfhip on this occafion, and jef-
" ftingly declared, that he fhould not be too fevere
" on the noble lord's meafures in America, for
" fear of lofing fo valuable a fupport. He con-
" cluded with trufting that the houfe would not,
" by a hafty decifion in favour of the petitioners,
" drive the planters to defperation." — Thus far Mr.
Fox.

It is impoffible to leave the caufe in better hands
than thofe of Mr. Fox. — The colonift, upon reading
this mafterly paffage, will naturally fay with a figh,
Oh! fi fic omnia.

Of

Of the Compacts subsisting between Great Britain and her Colonies.

Since the period of the American war, which has separated from us some of our principal colonies, without appearing much to diminish either our security or our prosperity; and, since a persuasion has taken place, that the East Indies are capable of furnishing us with sugar at reduced prices, a considerable number of persons (in which, perhaps, may be included several members of administation) have at once disputed the utility of our colonies, and started doubts as to their claims.* — It was natural, after disapproving an object, to get rid of the obstacles to discarding it. In this situation of things, then, several circumstances have occurred highly alarming to the colonists. — In the late debate upon the *sugar*-bill, a member high in office expressly declared, that he would never admit that any compact with the colonies existed, binding upon the mother-country; and another, no less eminent, intimated, that it was highly important that an early discussion should take place, respecting the mutual monopoly claimed by the sugar-

* See proofs of the late neglects shewn to the colonies very ably stated in *The Case of the Sugar-Colonies*, 1792, printed for Johnson and Debrett.

colonies.

colonies. — In the debates upon the *slave-trade*, which had preceded this discussion, it was held by several, with equal openness and decision, that this country was, in general, under no bond to give indemnity or even relief for most of the losses which might follow from the sudden abolition of the slave-trade. And, though some persons generously allowed that inquiry ought to be made into the justice of the claim, yet it is to be feared, that its large amount will of itself be a sufficient motive, with many, to question its validity; though it is clear that if it is of a magnitude too great to be supported by the *whole* of the British empire, it is certainly too oppressive to fail singly upon a part of it.—But, whatever may be the amount of these claims, it is here designed to discuss the solidity of their foundations; beginning more particularly with what respects the question respecting sugars.

Of the Compact respecting the double Monopoly.

Let us first, then, inquire into the nature of a compact, which, under whatever term signified, means a declaration, between two parties, of certain intentions, accompanied with more or less formality and explicitness, accordingly as the parties are respectively circumstanced in point of equality and confidence. If

the

the parties are enemies or ftrangers, the terms are not
fuppofed to have any force and effect till figned and
interchanged by the agents, and ratified by the princi-
pals. Between friends and perfons bound in a common intereft, lefs ceremony is neceffary, the common
bond fubfifting on each fide being ufually confidered as
comprehending and fuperceding every other. — But of
all compacts the leaft formal, but, at the fame time,
not the lefs facred, are thofe which occur between a
legiflature and its fubjects. When a government has
any thing to expect from a *fubject*, exprefs ftipulations
are entered into, becaufe the fubject is thought capable
of want of faith ; but, when the fubject has any thing to
expect from a legiflature, it is enough that the legiflature gives to its engagements the formality of a law ;
than which no obligation can be more imperative and
reftrictive upon the fubject, nor more binding to thofe
enacting it. As the whole power lies on one fide, fo
the law is expected to be obferved with a double portion of fcrupuloufnefs on the other. The compact (if
we venture to make a parallel in the only point in
which a parallel is admiffible) approaches to the nature of that taking place between the Divinity and
man; for which there are no parchments, no witnef-
fes, no fanctions, to produce, but fimply the folemn
declaration of a power having in view the happinefs of
the whole, and poffeffed of all the neceffary authority
for enforcing it.

If

If it be afked then, what compact exifts between the mother-country and its colonies? it is anfwered, that which is ufual between the powerful and weak, between patrons and their clients, between parents and their children; namely its *declaratians*. Some of the declarations of a legiflature are indeed by their very nature changeable. A civil regulation, a penal law, a military provifion, thefe and many other points are mutable in their very effence; becaufe the *end* alone of them is important, which is as explicit, generally, as it is important; and, becaufe the means for attaining this end are commonly capable of being varied, without diftreffing any honeft individual. The fame may be faid of other laws, where either the end or the means they have in view are *temporary*;—but where the end is of a different defcription, or where the means have of themfelves acquired magnitude enough to be confidered as an end, the queftion altogether affumes another complexion.

In the firft origin of a law, to inquire into the fincerity of the intentions of its framers would be deemed difrefpectful and idle; but, where time has rendered the law venerable, not by inattention or difufe, but by frequent recognition and inceffant practice; when it has been confirmed by fubfidiary provifions, applauded by parties who always differ upon other fubjects capable of difference, is taught in fchools, afferted by authors, univerfally imitated by neighbouring nations, and fealed by blood in many extenfive and burthenfome wars;

when

when the youngest and oldest of our living statesmen have been alike forward in its support; and when a property, equal in value to that of a third of the national debt, is built upon the basis of it; at such a period of the existence of the law, to express a doubt whether or not it has attained the essence and firmness of a compact, is to give suspicions, that it is a doubt of convenience rather than of system, of policy rather than of justice. — When the law recommends any enterprize, it is not of the nature of the recommendation of *one individual* to another, where the issue rests on the adopter of the advice, rather than on the giver; but when legislatures permit, and add recommendation to permission, they sanction and they promise; and, if the personal success of the enterprize lies with the party engaged in it, protection, at least, is solemnly pledged to it by the power framing the law.

This subject will be resumed upon general principles when we speak of what is due, in case of an abolition of the slave-trade; but, at present, it is time to refer to the long and solid tissue of law, respecting the double monopoly, subsisting between Great Britain and the West Indies; each portion of which tissue derives force from its connection with others, and no part of it is stronger than that which has been latest framed. For this purpose the reader is desired seriously to consult the paper contained in the *Appendix*, intitled, the Legal Claim, &c.

G

To

To the hoft of laws there cited, a multitude of others might have been added; and it is believed that a challenge may be given to any one to find a fingle law contravening their general fpirit in the whole ftatute-book, at leaft in modern times; or yet a fingle claufe expreffing an intimation, that the fyftem contained in them was either limited, temporary, or in the ftyle of an experiment; obfervations which will appear ftill more forcible, when we confider the laws refpecting the flave-trade.—The paper in queftion is known to have been very fuddenly drawn up; and, fince its adoption by the Weft-India meeting, a fentence has been inferted by its author, which will be found included in brackets in its 6th page.

After a perufal of this paper, of which the purport (till the period that has been mentioned) has been confirmed by every fpecies of conference with adminiftration from time immemorial, as well as by every debate in parliament, the reader will determine whether men of plain fenfe, fuch as are fit for colonizing and for merchandize, can have extracted any other meaning from the fpirit of the laws in queftion, than that which they have adopted; and whether blame can reft upon them for having gradually ftaked feventy millions fterling on their pledge, except upon the ground of their having had too eafy a faith in any thing belonging to politics; a cenfure to which they may be forced to yield,

without

without its ferving as any juftification to thofe who fhall opprefs them.

We fhall fucceffively bring other arguments into view, refpecting the claim of the coloniſts to a doublɘ monopoly, in the courfe of anſwering the following objections. For example,

I. It is faid that *free trade* has great merits.

Perhaps there is no perfon, who is more deeply convinced of the importance of a free trade to the arts, civilization, profperity, and univerfal fraternity of mankind, than the author of thefe remarks. He is even ready to allow, that the Weſt-India colonies have been built on two falfe principles: firſt, flavery, with its unfortunate companion the flave-trade; and, fecondly,. a reciprocal monopoly. But thefe principles were Britifh in their origin, not colonial. We now fee the error on all fides: — but what is to be done? — To fpeak at prefent only of that refpecting the *monopoly*, had the colonifts fet off fairly, none would have embarked or continued in the iflands, but upon principles which experimentally would have defied foreign rivalfhip of all forts. An artificial fyſte·   ·wever, was fubftituted: we planned, and the co.   executed; and, if we defert them, they muſt ne...farily become the victims. Property in the iflands has fhifted hands fo often, that eftates ftand chiefly on the bafis of purchafe at *forced* prices, or, if we pleafe to ufe the term, at *patent* prices, inftead of running in lines of family defcent; and

thefe

thefe prices were *prices forced by the fyftem which Great
Britain has enacted.*

But it may be faid, are things never to change ? —
Yes, if a change is wanted, nothing is neceffary but
time. The ferment is rapidly at work: *the opinion of
your juftice is greatly fhaken:* eftates in the Weft Indies, as has been obferved, are not, as in England,
matters of pride and of inheritance, but objects of trade;
and, in the circulation of them, Weft-India property
will foon arrive at a truer level. Men will arrange their
family affairs, and merchants will lend their money,
with a view to the new fyftem;—but it is unjuft to the
laft degree to precipitate this procefs, which, after all,
is only rendering the injury gradual, inftead of fudden.
In fhort, their golden days are over in the iflands, and
we wifh to end their iron days by the abolition of the
flave-trade, and to bring them back to days of inno-
cence and peace, but we take care they fhall not be
piping days. We have, *in effect,* faid of the colony-
fyftem, (as it will foon be proved that we've *exprefsly*
faid of the flave-fyftem,) what we do at prefent of our
own conftitution; we have faid of each, *efto perpetua!*
Let us not then repent in anger and in rafhnefs, but remember the maxim *feftina lente,* and ufe a gentle fpeed,
a cautious hafte. Even this will violate our faith to
thofe who keep and to thofe who fell eftates, as well as
to their creditors; and will only be harmlefs to the new
buyers of eftates.— But, as the refolution of perfons in

power

power feems now to be taken, to affume the lion's fhare
of all which is here in difpu...; nothing feems to remain
for the colonies but the choice of the eafieft ruin,
which feems to be that here alluded to.

II. But it will be faid, that the *mutual* monopoly,
claimed by the Weft Indies, is unfair; fince it is not a
monopoly which is *mutually equal.* — It would take
long to difcufs this queftion; and, after what has juft
been faid, it feems a fuperfluous difcuffion. Befides, it
muft be recollected, that, on our fide, we have fuper-
added a claim to make *commercial regulations* for the
colonies, independent of thofe which relate to the monopoly; a claim which has been attended in its exercife with confiderable rigours; of which the abolition
of the flave-trade, when accomplifhed, will probably
ferve as a memorable example, and which, therefore,
muft count for fomething in the balance.

But let what follows be coolly confidered. — Taking
one year with another for twenty years together, the
intereft of the money, gained upon a given capital in
the iflands, is extremely moderate. At the fame
time, the natural inftability of colonial property is
fuch, that eftates are fold for twelve or fourteen years
purchafe. In war, there are great anxieties occurring
from the enemy; in peace, as well as war, great caufe
of uneafinefs is now to be expected from an innovating
legiflature at home; at all times there is a frequent ab-
fence, from friends and connections, requifite; and the
                                                        lofs

lofs of health is fo notorious, that the gains of the colonift ought to be rapidly acquired, in order to cor-
refpond with the rapid wafte of life which occurs in
attaining them. Befides, it is a very true, though a
very old, remark, that the colony-wealth becomes
the wealth of the mother-country; and not only en-
riches our traders, but raifes the purchafe of our lands,
and yields a valuable article to exchange with foreign
nations, to fay nothing of our navy

But, if the monopoly fhall at any time be withdrawn
from the colonifts, it muft, at the fame time, be
equally renounced by Great Britain. On the fide of
Great Britain, however, the complete abandonment of
the fyftem will be peculiarly difficult; fince there are
few articles belonging to her, which monopoly does
not, in fome fhape or other, invade, fo as to enhance
the coft of moft of the articles which fhe furnifhes. —
In the mean time, one cannot but fmile at the impa-
tience with which this fyftem is adhered to by the nation, refpecting its colonies, while it fubmits to its ty-
ranny in a multitude of other important inftances, without murmur, or even notice.*

III. But

* " The indifference with which fome treat the obligation in
" the compact, for the fyftem of reciprocal monopoly, on the
" fide of Great Britain, makes it neceffary to notice the rigour
" with which an obfervance of it is neverthelefs enforced upon
" the colonies. Not only the colonift is obliged to depofit, in a
" ftate

III. But it is objected more particularly, and even tauntingly, that our colonifts furnifh the articles they supply

" ftate particularly fubject to lofs by drainage and to expence of
" carriage, the chief of his produce for fale in Great Britain, but
" he is reftricted to Great Britain for his principal purchafes, and
" to Britifh fhips for his fole conveyances, even in time of war,
" when he might avail himfelf both of the cheapnefs and conve-
" nience of neutral bottoms. He is allowed indeed to purchafe
" building-timber, packages, live ftock, and certain articles of pro-
" vifion, from the neighbouring continent of North America: but
" though, from the circumftances of the iflands, his wants of thefe
" articles are progreffively multiplying, he muft obtain them under
" fuch difadvantages, that, when the obftacles attending the fale
" of his melaffes and rum are confidered, it is 100 per cent. be-
" yond their price before the American war, and 50 per cent. be-
" yond the prices at which rival colonies may obtain them. It
" happens unfortunately, alfo, that the fame caufes, which produce
" a fhortnefs of crops, commonly occafion an increafe of expences,
" from an accompanying dearth of provifions. And yet this mo-
" nopoly-fyftem is fo rigidly purfued by Great Britain, that not
" only the convenience and the neceffities of the iflands have given
" way to it, but a facrifice to our navigation-laws has even been
" made of the *lives* of thofe negroes whofe happinefs is the pre-
" tended object of many who clamour againft the colonifts. Such
" is a part of the price, then, which the planter pays for the benefit
" of an exclufive market in the mother-country, the comparative
" value of which is yearly declining by the price of fugar rifing in
" foreign colonies. It would be hard indeed, therefore, after fub-
" jecting him to regulations, which, however beneficial they may
" be thought to the mother-country, are, in too many inftances,
" and in an increafing degree, oppreffive to the colonies, if he is
" to

supply on dearer terms than thofe of other nations. ——
Their articles, however, cannot be greatly dearer;
becaufe we have always exported refined fugars to
contend with the fugars of foreign colonifts. It is true,
that, during many years paft, the real bounty, given
upon refined fugars, powerfully fupported our colonifts
in this rivalfhip. The intrinfic difproportion of price
in fugars, however, has, of late, gradually diminifhed;

" to be deprived of the benefit of a fluctuation of prices, from
" which, at times, he muft neceffarily be the fufferer."
    " Between the years 1780 and 1787 the ifland of Jamaica loft
" 15,000 negroes from famine, or bad provifions, and confequent
" difeafes, befides fimilar mifchiefs in fome of the other iflands.
" Provifions, however, are a neceffary of life, and fugar is not a
" neceffary; the price of provifions alfo was, in various cafes,
" quadrupled to the colonifts at fome moments, and fugar has
" fcarcely doubled its price in England; the laws reftricting the
" American intercourfe are permanent, and the inconvenience re-
" fpecting the price of fugar is temporary; laftly, much difficulty,
" arifing from the reftrictions to the intercourfe between the United
" States and the Britifh Weft-Indies, was forefeen, but the na-
" tural and political calamities operating upon the price of fugar
" are fuch as are wholly unprecedented in the nature of human af-
" fairs."
    " In the numerous wars in which Great Britain has engaged,
" and of which they have borne more than their proportion both of
" the evil and of the burthen, though they have often been the
" prize contended for, they have never been the origin of the con-
" tention." — *Weft-India Memorial to Miniftry, February 28, 1792.*

and,

and, at the prefent inftant, Britifh fugars have become
cheaper than thofe of France, even allowing for the
difference of French exchange.* — The refult of thefe
comparifons is the more favourable to the Britifh colonift, as he had fuffered greatly by the ravages of the
late war, and found the Britifh market bare of fugars
after the war; and has fince had armaments, hurricanes, and other natural calamities, to alarm the buyers or to render his fupplies fcanty, befides the difadvantages incurred by his being now more reftrained
as to the American intercourfe, than the French colonift. In fhort, befides fupplying the Britifh and Irifh
confumption, an exportation of our fugar has always
exifted; and the real embarraffment of government,
during the late controverfies about fugar, chiefly arofe
from a fudden exportation, which caufed large amounts
of the fugar-tax to be refunded; and the remedy, firft
thought of for the evil, was ftopping that exportation:
— fo that though we have had, as is well known, an
increafing confumption at home, yet we have ftill received fugars enough for ourfelves and fome for our
neighbours.

The objection however, before us, will not be fatif-
factorily anfwered, without faying a word or two on

* To make this argument of fome effect, it muft be remarked,
that, notwithftanding the convulfions in the French iflands, they have
ftill furnifhed more than enough fugar to France for its home confumption.

the

the comparative state of the British and French sugar-colonies; — the fundamental difference between which appears to respect their *soil*. Land has only *gradually* offered itself for cultivation on our side: and therefore (for a reason given before, namely, *bavit*) has been constantly dear; for it will be remembered, that our original stock of land was first increased by the treaty of Utrecht in 1713; next, in 1740, by a treaty with the Maroon negroes in Jamacia, which tranquillized and admitted of cultivation in an immense tract of country; and, lastly, by the several valuable islands ceded by the French at the peace of 1763. — The French, on their side, have obtained their lands cheap, by having had a vast field opened at *once*, as well as from having the prospect of large additions at Cayenne, and the possibility of acquiring even the Spanish part of St. Domingo (which is twice as large as their own part). Land too with them was at all times distributed *gratis* to new settlers; and exemptions from various burthens during a course of years were superadded in their favour. The soil also, generally speaking, was far more fertile than ours; which not only allowed of the general advantages attending that circumstance, but admitted of the particular system of ratoons, that is, of a crop of young canes springing annually from the old roots.* It has before been observed,

that

* This saved the labour of planting annually, as well as what is to be deemed equivalent to a loss by fallow; the plants requiring

fourteen

that French raw fugar is inferior in quality to ours; a circumftance which is certainly to be counted (though it
has generally been forgotten) in the comparifon of
prices. Their white fervants alfo are cheaper; their
negroes, though dearly bought, are more feverely
worked; and, of late, they have had the benefit of a
freer intercourfe with North America, than we have
allowed our own colonies. Their courfe for navigation
alfo in various refpects is better circumftanced. But
what perhaps, above all, contributed moft to their late
fuperiority, was the eminent advantage poffeffed in
various particulars by the colony of St. Domingo;
among which may be reckoned, the cheapnefs of its
cattle, and the facility of other lucrative trade, particularly for bullion, owing to the contiguity of the
Spaniards: and the great influence of this immenfe
colony, in bearing down the price of the produce of
the fmaller French iflands, (which muft have been
chiefly effected by keeping down the value of their
foil,) will readily be acknowledged. It is but candid
however to allow, that the French colonifts have enjoyed no fuperiority whatever in point of freight, nor
till of late have they been fairly dealt with as to their
rum.—If the French fpend lefs money in their fugar-
buildings, and are more frequently refident on the fpot

fourteen months growth, and the ratoons (or *rejettons*) only twelve;
without being attended with a proportionate difference of produce,
all things confidered.

than

than our colonifts, it is a reproach, rather than an ex-
cufe, to the latter; fince thefe are benefits which are
certainly equally acceffible on their fide, had there been
a difpofition to feek them.

Of the Compact refpecting the African Slave-Trade.

Our legiflature has encouraged the Weft-India colonies to raife produce, not only for the home-market,
for Ireland, and for our other colonies, but alfo, in the
moft exprefs manner, for the fupply of *foreign* nations.
Of this the references in the Appendix will furnifh
various proofs; though none other is wanting than the
fact of a drawback and even a bounty having, for many years, down to the prefent period, been given on the
exportation of *fugar* to foreign parts.—But, at the fame
time that we have encouraged production as an end,
we expreffly encouraged the importation of African flaves
as the *means*; and we even thought the trade in them
fo innocent, that we were anxious to become pur-
veyors of them to foreigners; as witnefs the memorable proceedings refpecting the Affiento treaty. — Our
encouragement here was general, without limit as to
time or as to numbers. One charter, (granted to the
Duke

Duke of York, and two of our queens, in partnerſhip with ſeveral others,* under the name of the *Royal Ad-venturers,)* which contained a clauſe for conveying three thouſand negroes annually to the Weſt Indies, was for the term of *one thouſand years.* Two acts of parliament on this ſubject will be found cited in the Appendix, pages 5 & 6, and their preambles (which are there given) leave no doubt as to the full adoption of the principle as applied to the Weſt Indies; and it is only by late deciſions that the property in negro ſlaves was determined not to ſubſiſt in Great Britain. — The act, of 23 Geo. II. ch. 31. which declares that the African trade was merely *advantageous* to Great Britain, but was *neceſſary* to ſupply a ſufficient number of negroes to the colonies at reaſonable rates; enacts, that the ſaid trade between Barbary and the Cape of Good Hope ſhall be open to *all* his majeſty's ſubjects, when and at ſuch times and in ſuch manner as they ſhall think fit,

---

* A noble lord has played with ſucceſs on the charter and laws here cited. — His *dramatis perſonæ*, however, as to the charter, might have been heightened by the mention of the two queens. The ſucceſs under this charter was ſuch as may be expected when Royal Adventurers engage in trade; but the charter, it muſt be remembered, was granted to the Duke of York by Charles II. in whoſe reign were paſſed moſt of the laws on which our colonial ſyſ-tem is founded. — It is farther ſingular, that the paſſages referred to, in the act immediately to be cited, (23 Geo. II. chap. 31,) have been overlooked on both ſides; though the act has repeated-ly been publicly noticed on both ſides in the controverſy on the ſlave-trade.

without

without any reſtraint whatever (ſave as therein after is
expreſſed); and *all* ſuch traders are *for ever* thereafter
to be incorporated by the name of the Company of
Merchants trading to Africa, and are, by the ſame
name, to have *perpetual ſucceſſion.* It is true, that the
29th clauſe of this act prohibits *kidnapping* of the na-
tives, but it does ſo without teaching any abhorrence of
the ſlave-trade; for it is only ſaid, that this ſhall not
be done *to the prejudice of the ſaid trade,* in conſe-
quence of which, half of the penalty of one hundred
pounds goes to the company, for maintaining the African forts; which, almoſt without exception, were
deſtined to protect the ſlave-trade, and which are to
this hour ſupported for the ſame purpoſe by annual
grants from the Britiſh parliament.——After theſe ſpe-
cimens, we ſhall take no farther trouble in citing char-
ters, parliamentary proceedings, or national treaties
and meaſures, on this ſubject, the principle in queſtion
being eſtabliſhed paſt the poſſibility of diſpute.

The ſlave-trade, thus in effect granted without
limits to the colonies. has, however, been attempted to be limited by the colonies themſelves, and
in particular by thoſe ſituated upon the North A-
merican continent;* but altogether in vain, on account

* This aſſertion is made upon no leſs authority than that of Dr.
Franklin, and it will be confirmed by the following citation from
Anderſon's Hiſtory of Commerce, 4to edition, vol. 3, p. 191.
" The

count of the superior influence of the African merchants, who have oppofed the king's affent to fuch
laws. Mr. Dundas's well-judged propofal, that no
aged negroes fhould be imported into our colonies,
has long been anticipated by the legiflature of Jamaica,
which paffed a law to that effect in 1772; but, to this
law, the king's fanction was refufed in 1774, after a
formal hearing before the privy council, owing to the
interference above alluded to. — Thus circumftanced,
then, were the colonifts waranted to fufpect any fcru-
ples in the Britifh legiflature on a fubject, where what
is right to-day cannot be wrong to-morrow, but one
unvariable principle muft at all times decide?

As to *morality* on this occafion, the colonifts have
at all times viewed it through the medium of the mother-country. The Britifh laws are not merely trading
laws: our legiflature is a cenfor of morals, and even a
fuperintender of religion, not only prohibiting fabbath-
breaking, wanton fwearing, and the like; but even
fcrutinizing into the fpecies of religion adopted by its
fubjects; which may be feen as well in the cafe of
the teft-laws, as in the horrid ftatutes, for whofe repeal
Mr. Fox lately moved in the Houfe of Commons.
The king, who forms one branch of the legiflature,

" The following *complaint* has lately been made to the board
" trade and plantations, viz. In New York there is a duty of two
" pounds laid on all negroes imported from Africa, and of four..
" pounds on all negroes imported from any other place. is

is the fupreme head of our national church; and all
the reverend prelates of the realm make part of another
branch (where alfo judges are conftantly affifting, fkill-
ed in the principles of natural law and natural right,
for the purpofe of aiding its counfels.)—Indeed the
very attempt now carrying on in the legiflature for the
abolition of the flave-trade, what is it, but a fuppofed meafure of humanity and juftice ; and therefore befitting its attention? as was, nearly in fo many
words, fignified by the Commons to the Lords, at a
late conference, appointed for that purpofe.* Laws
paffed and proceedings had, under all thefe circumftances,
during near a century and a half, cannot but have marked the moral fentiments, as well as the political opinion, of the legiflature upon this fubject.—The colonifts therefore, in this trade, have only been paffive:
we provided negroes, and they bought them; in fhort,

* The fociety for propagating the gofpel in foreign parts has given
its fanction in like manner with the preceding refpectable perfonages to colonial flavery; in confequence of having poffeffed property
cultivated by flaves and added to the number of them by purchafe,
as well as of having leafed their land to others to be tilled by flaves,
in order with the returns produced thence to teach the *Chriftian faith*.
Blackftone, fays, that *Chriftianity is part of the laws of
England*; and accordingly his firft chapter on offences refpects
thofe againft God and religion. Will any one, then, after reading that curious chapter, afirm, that parliament is to be deemed
not to have taken cognizance of the morality of the flave-trade and
of flavery till the prefent moment ?

they

they bought both negroes and estates, each requiring
large additions of other negroes, because the authorities
constituted for that purpose, pronounced it lawful for
a *thousand years* to come, and even *for ever*.

Has the above right, then, of acquiring negroes at
any time been forfeited? — Let us boldly open the dif-
cussion, which the sagacity of the persons espousing the
opposite party will not suffer to escape them. — We
may observe, then, upon this subject, as follows.
First, the colonists have gone upon the following plan,
which is the plan of every great city; namely, to im-
port their labourers, rather than to breed them; and,
as they imported them for working in the field, they
naturally chose (as we do whenever the occasion juf-
tifies a difference) men, rather than women. Hence
an inequality between the sexes, which polygamy con-
curred to aggravate; and the remainder of the men
becoming thus still more disproportionate in number
to the women, licentiousness and its attendant diseases
followed, as usual in such cases, to the certain obstruc-
tion of population. Secondly, it will not be imputed
as a crime to the colonists to have been unable to cure
or prevent the propagation of certain African diseases,
as they have in vain employed a numerous and skilful
band of medical persons for that purpose. Neither
is it their crime, that children, in spite of all their
efforts, find a particular day succeeding their birth, too
often becoming fatal to them; a plain proof that fe-

I   verity

verity has no fhare in fuch mortality. Neither yet is it their crime not to have confidered the flave- as in a point of view, in which we have never ourfelves confidered it till within thefe four years; and refpecting which we had not favoured them with the flighteft warning, not having fent even proper clergymen among them to enlighten and improve them.

As to their *Laws*, whether cruel or whether mild, our king and privy council have fanctioned every one of them; without which fanction none would have been valid, and refpecting which fanction many members of the privy council, now preffing for the abolition of flave-trade, will find themfelves deeply committed. — If obfolete laws, however, are to be deemed the type of the feeling and practice of a country, with what felf-reproach muft we not look at our *own* ftatute-book, where fectaries are often found confidered as deferving more ignominious and ftricter treatment than negro-flaves?* But, that fuch laws are not to be confidered

as

---

* Profecutions on the fubject of witchcraft were only put an end to by 9 Geo. II. chap. 5; the laws on that fubject having been proved, not many years before, *not* to have been fleeping laws.

As an eminent leader in the Houfe of Commons, not lefs remarkable for his candour than his fagacity, has cenfured the Weft Indians for drawing an argument from what happens as to witchcraft in Africa; it is proper to remark, that they only affirm that perfons are there *punifhed* for witchcraft; though they might add, that, under the *cloak* of witchcraft, various arts are practifed; fuch as

exciting

as so indicative in the opinion of the House of Commons, and especially of its great leader, as also of the bishops, we may conclude, from their not concurring with Mr. Fox in a wish for an immediate repeal of all such, or even of the worst of them. Besides, Jamaica passed its great act for amending its slave-laws, spontaneously and upon its own suggestion, before the subject underwent a parliamentary discussion here; and several of the islands, particularly Grenada and Jamaica, have since passed, or are passing, acts for producing still farther amendments; each overlooking that *danger of circumstances* arising from the feelings of the slaves at this critical juncture, which, by the same precedent of the House of Commons, respecting a reform in religious as well as civil matters, it seems might have been procrastinated or modified without meriting censure.

But the actual *conduct* of the colonists to the negroes may be said to become a fair object of inquiry. — But has it not always been open to inquiry? Have their clergy, who are all appointed by the crown; has their diocesan, the bishop of London; have those other dignitaries in the society for propagating the gospel in foreign parts; have these ever remonstrated with them

exciting terror in the mind, and giving drugs (which are often fatal) to affect the body, of which many instances are exhibited among the negroes in the West Indies. — But it is enough for them to prove that witchcraft is *believed* without proving that it is *real*.

I 2

upon

upon this fubject? Have our governors, and military and other officers, ever formally complained of them? — Hear what our governors and officers have ftated in evidence at the bar of both of our Houfes of Parliament, as well as to the king in privy council; and diftinguifh carefully between their *evidence* as to facts, and their *opinions* as to confequences; obferving that the firft cannot eafily be miftaken, whatever may be thought of the fecond. It is true, indeed, that fome have infinuated, that the colonifts have always affumed a caution refpecting their flaves in the prefence of thefe refpectable perfonages; but is it not idle to fuppofe, that concealment can have been fuccefsful with perfons confiderable in number, and feveral of whom have viewed the iflands in various capacities; or that fuch perfons fhould not, even in their journies, have been able to take cruelty by furprize, if it had been general? — But we fay, that at leaft fome of our colonifts have incurred guilt by their oppreffions. Agreed; but have *all* of them done fo? Have their abfent merchants, their mortgagees, and other creditors, or the foreigners who have lent them money, been partakers in it? — Punifh the guilty; give to *them* perfonally no indemnity:—but do not meafure the guilt of any by their want of fuccefs in keeping up their population; a criterion, which it would be hard to reft upon too far, at the moment when we fay that their loffes are in general fo nearly fupplied by breeding, that they

may

may now furrender the refource of importation without much inconvenience.

Laftly, it may be queried, Whether the *nature* of the injury, which the colonifts are like to fuftain by a fuppreffion of flave-trade, is fuch as fuperfedes their title to indemnity ? — And to this I anfwer, that their agricultural eftablifhments are, by their nature, permanent, efpecially that part of them which confifts in the foil ; alfo that they are not convertible to other objects ; and that they are of large amount as to value, and have become the fubject of pledges to many. The fugar-cane, in particular, requires large manufactories for making either raw or clayed fugar, as well as for rum ; and to thefe muft be added other buildings formed in confequence ; as alfo aqueducts, refervoirs, roads, &c. &c.

It is by fome, indeed, argued, that men muft expect a fluctuation in the laws of all countries. — This may be true, where the object is fluctuating ; but permanent objects require permanent laws, efpecially where they are of a magnitude to form general fyftems. They are defigned to fpeak in plain terms to unlettered men, and to prompt and guide them in their actions ; and, where ages have elapfed, practice becomes a proof, as well as a facred warrant of the intention. — To give a contrary account of the legiflation, is to make it a monfter, ruin attends whofe motions. It is giving to legiflators themfelves the following language :

language : " Beware of us, you who are subject to
" us: we have not only the power, but the caprice,
" of tyrants: we encourage to day and open to you
" the long *vijto* of for ever, and to-morrow we re-
" tract and dig a gulph to overwhelm you: we
" urge and we recall: we expect every thing from
" you, and are bound to nothing for ourselves." ——
What trade or agriculture can support this verfatility
and want of principle? And who will rifk their lives
and health under fuch a legiflature?—Money, depo-
fited in national funds, is notorioufly liable to uncertainties, and becomes a fpecies of gambling; but,
when the fatal blank occurs, it is there the act of
neceffity. But here no pecuniary neceffity being
pleaded, meafures of municipal law demand the utmoft ftability, juftice, and clearnefs. — We may
venture, therefore, to affert, that, if the fund for creating an indemnity were obtainable at free coft, from
other quarters, none would doubt as to the principle
here contended for ..—to be convinced of which, let us
only look at our own conduct at home. When Mr.
Burke wifhed to abolifh offices ufelefs and even dangerous, he faid, compenfate; when Mr. Pitt former-
ly defired to extinguifh the rotten boroughs, he faid,
compenfate; and the fame was Mr. Dundas's language, with refpect to the African fhips, in cafe of
abolifhing the flave-trade; though thefe fhips were
neceffarily temporary, and perifhing in their nature;

as

as well as convertible to other objects. Shall we protect, then, only the inhabitants of Great Britain? Is it
true with us, that to be removed from fight is to be
removed from care? Is it juft to rob Peter to pay
Paul? Impoffible. — Our colonifts did, indeed, hold
themfelves bound to fubmit to loffes from war, and
from foreign rivaifhip occurring in foreign markets, and
even from the interfeience of lands which might hereafter be ceded for the purpofe of enlarging our fettlements;
but the abolition of the flave-trade, they were never pre-
pared for, after we had fo folemnly eftablifhed, ratified,
and even fanctioned, it. — Can any thing more ftrong-
ly prove, that we are proceeding upon an innovation,
when we hear, as a part of the new doctrines, that
*no increafe whatever of cultivation is henceforth to be
provided for;* a pofition, uttered at the very moment
when the colonies were reproached with not fupplying our markets fufficiently with fugar. —— Why
did former laws, in an unlimited manner, encourage
the pufhing forwards of fettlements? Why did the
crown throw new lands into circulation? Why did they
make the fettlers purchafe them at a heavy expence in
the ceded iflands? And, Why were penalties affixed to
delays attending their cultivation?

In fhort, there is no end to the crowd of arguments
which offer on this fubject : — yet every thing which
can be faid, on this fide of the water, falls fhort
of the ftatements which will foon reach us from the
other

other fide, where the amount of the intended grievance
alone can be fully known, becaufe there alone it can be
fully felt. Few, indeed, are the eftates where negroes
are not wanted; and many are thofe perfons, who poffefs
tracts of land upon which cultivation has not yet be-
gun; and ftill more are thofe who poffefs eftates whofe
cultivation is ftill incomplete. — The moft vigorous
powers of calculation and reafoning, when applied to
imperfect data, only lead to ingenious modes of error;
and if facts, therefore, fhall prove the depopulation of
the iflands to be in general confiderable, we muft bow
to facts rather than to oppofing authorities, however
brilliant and however well-intentioned. — To conclude
this argument; if a grievance fhall be created, by the
abolition of the flave-trade, it becomes this country to
provide the remedy, or elfe an indemnity for what cannot be remedied.

At prefent, all that is neceffary is to deprecate the
announcing of hoftile opinions and adopting of prejudices upon this fubject. — For myfelf, I cannot difap-
prove the conduct of thofe who wifh to terminate the
flave-trade; and I think that it ought to be done without reference to its impreffion upon the Britifh empire
or to its expence; becaufe the unhappy Africans, who
are the victims of it, were not parties to the engagements refpecting themfelves, made between us and our
colonies. If the African potentates could now be made
parties to the plan of abolition, I fhould farther fay that
the

the abolition ought to be immediate. — But whenever
the abolition ihall once be decided upon, then com-
mences the queftion of compenfation; which certainly
ought to be made to fit as light as poffible upon the
mother-country; and it is even fair to add, that fome
of the burthen of fo neceffary a work may fairly reft
with the colonifts, as forming part of the empire at large.

A few meafures in the way of relief, not very
difficult to adopt, on the part of Great Britain, and
which are independant of the recourfe to be had to
pecuniary compenfation will now be mentioned. 1°.
The habitual reliance of the colonifts on the benefits of
the Britifh markets muft on no account be wantonly
checked. 2°. New burthens muft not be impofed, at
the prefent moment, to opprefs the colonifts. Thus
far is negative. But, 3°. as the colonifts are expected
to facrifice their faireft hopes and perhaps their
poffeffions on the altar of humanity, England her-
felf muft facrifice fomething on the fame altar, by
relaxing in her feverity as to the interdiction of the
North-American trade. If the Weft Indies were not
fettled on the exprefs *promife* of this intercourfe being
continued to them under every *poffible* circumftance;
yet they certainly proceeded upon the *faith* of it; and
it is for a very peculiar reafon neceffary to them on the
prefent occafion. It is not merely from the trite confideration of economy, or even of plentiful and feafon-
able fupplies, particularly in cafe of famine or war,

K   that

that the negroes may be said to depend upon it; but it
is important in the view of leaving as little as possible
for *slaves* to perform, and of transfering their task as much
as possible to *freemen*; for, if the slaves are confined to
the cultivation of products peculiar to the tropics, their
labour is thus best employed, and may then be exchan-
ged with advantage for the produce of other climates
inhabited by freemen; and thus give to Great Britain
an increase of colony-products independent of any
augmentation of slavery. This suggestion should be
listened to with the more attention, as our present policy
on the subject of America has by no means succeeded
to us; for, in consequence of shutting the Americans
out of the West Indies, they have only crept into the
East Indies, to the diminution of our own trade to
America, and the increase of the clandestine conveyance of India goods into our own islands; and they
have also resorted to manufactures and a system of re-
taliation, which would otherwise have been left unat-
tempted. As this intercourse is now said to be under
negotiation, and as we may obtain some equivalent by
conceding it as a favour; it will not farther be pressed
for here as a spontaneous act towards the colonies.
4°. Indented servants, or, if we please, freemen, must
as much as possible be introduced into the islands; in
order to render it possible to turn their negro domestics
and tradesmen into the field, as an aid to the present
stock of field labourers, Europeans, for various
reasons,

reafons, are out of the queſtion; and at preſent it may
be a critical matter to attempt the ſearch of indented
ſervants or freemen in *Africa*; but, without ſpeaking
alſo of the *Hindoos*, is it not perfectly practicable to
obtain a number of *Chineſe* fit for the purpoſe? The
Chineſe are much given to expatriate; they are an
ingenious, laborious, and frugal, people; they underſtand how to relieve the inconveniences and add to
the enjoyments of a hot climate; they would ſerve not
only as domeſtic ſervants, but as tradeſmen and ſuper-
intendants; they are to be found in every quarter of
the *Eaſt-India iſlands*, wherever an European factory is
eſtabliſhed; they are not afraid of croſſing the ſea,
which they frequent in the Company's ſervice; and,
before many years elapſe, it will be found eaſy, perhaps, to have prevailed upon an amount of one or two
hundred thouſand of them, of different ſexes, to mi-
grate to our iſlands. In this very important experiment the concurrence of government is indiſpenſable;
and we may add, at the ſame time, that this is owing to
the colonies, ſhould the ſlave-trade be aboliſhed; and,
as far as it went, it would be an indemnity *in kind*; and
even conſtitute a benefit, as the parties brought might
be depended upon for contributing to defend the iſlands
both againſt their external and internal enemies. 5°. The
iſlands may be eſſentially ſerved, alſo, by the introduction of various plants. The bread-fruit will be a noble
preſent, and the various ſpice-trees a politic one: the

ſeveral

feveral fpecies of bamboo, alfo, will not be without
their ufe; and the introduction of Eaftern fruits might
add to the temptation in favour of refidence in the
iflands. Perhaps it might not be fuperfluous to make
trial of new fpecies of the *fugar-cane,* of which there are
feveral afcertained, though one only is known to our
iflands, the whole ftock of what we poffefs (if we are
to pay attention to learned botanifts) being to be confidered as various parts of one identical plant, in confequence of having been propagated from ftems and
roots, inftead of feeds. 6°. Among other new importations, ufeful animals fhould not be forgotten;
whether for labour, as the Eaftern bullock, or for food,
or other ferviceable purpofes. — Thefe feveral means
of relief could not be very coftly, but might prove
highly efficacious; and contribute to the benefit
of others befides the actual fufferers, as well as
to the ornament and reputation of our age and
nation. — Indemnities of a *mere direct* kind muft be
left to the juftice and generofity of the Britifh nation,
when a proper period fhall arrive for confidering this
important fubject.

We fhall now conclude with two or three mifcel-
laneous obfervations refpecting the flave-queftion.

I. The *right* of Great Britain to controul and even
abolifh the flave-trade, provided fhe makes due compenfation

penſation to the coloriſts, has never hitherto been conteſted — A great law perſonage, in the Houſe of Lords, has lately thought proper to ſtart a doubt upon this ſubject, which may have conſiderable influence in exciting a regular oppoſition upon this ground in the iſlands. The coloriſts, however, will ſuffer ſo much by the abolition of the ſlave-trade, that it is hoped that no new calamity will be coupled with it, ariſing from a political diſpute, founded ſolely in miſtake, and for which it is impoſſible to chooſe a time more dangerous than the preſent; whether we conſider their domeſtic ſituation, or the novel poſition of their commerce.

The claim of this country to regulate the commerce of the colonies, is co-eval with their ſettlement, and was acknowledged even by thoſe among them which denied our right to taxation. It is clear, indeed, that this power muſt reſide ſomewhere; and, as no conſtitutional proviſion whatever is made for a joint exerciſe of it, it naturally follows, that, from the earlieſt ſettlers, down to the lateſt, every man is bound by the claims which have been inſtituted by the mothercountry, from the earlieſt moment, and which have, in effect, been made the baſis and condition of our connection.

As the law of England, as well as natural law, when giving a right, give alſo every thing that is neceſſary to the full exerciſe of that right, ſo in the
preſent

prefc.... inftance we find, that, at the earlieft periods, cuftom-houfe officers have been appointed, and cuftom-houfe dues been received in the colonies, by virtue of Englifh laws. The declaratory act, in 1766, which affumed the right of binding the colonies in all cafes whatfoever, will not be brought in argument on this occafion; becaufe every thing, which pretends to too much authority, is apt, at laft, to become no authority for any thing;—but we may fairly cite the act, in 1778, which *renounced taxation* over the colonies, becaufe the provifions of this colony-*Magna-Charta* were never objected to in any reprefentations made by the colonifts, either at home or abroad. By this act, a *referve* of power is exprefly made for impofing fuch duties, as may be expedient for the *regulation of commerce*; the *nett* * produce of fuch duties to be always paid and applied to the ufe of the colony in which the fame fhall be refpectively levied, in fuch manner as other duties, collected by the authority of its General Affembly, are ordinarily paid and applied. Purfuant to this principle, the free-port acts have conftantly levied upon the colonies all the fums neceffary for carrying the fame into effect; and to this example, which is frefh in memory, a multitude of others may be added, were not the principle too univerfally acknowledged to want any confirmation.

* That is, after paying the charges attending the carrying fuch regulations into execution.

Unhappily

Unhappily the purchase and the importation of slaves
in the colonies are too certainly to be contemplated
as a *trade*; and though the propriety of this term has
been difputed by thofe who wifh for the abolition, yet
the acts of parliament confirming it, and the colonifts,
at all times, when fpeaking of it, declare it to be a
trade; and therefore confefs it to be fubject to regulation by the Britifh parliament. — But the fubmiffion of
the colonies to this authority in queftion ftands on a
much more folid ground than mere implication. In
the courfe of the laft four years, the colonies, either
by themfelves, their agents, or fome of the moft refpectable individuals among them, have confented or
requefted to be examined on the part of one or other
of the *three* branches of our legiflature, in confequence
of the motions for the abolition of the flave-trade having been repeatedly announced and debated in parliament. This *acquiefcence*, in the power of our legiflature, on this fubject, has been too marked and repeat-
ed not to compromife and bind the colonies, and to
prevent all controverfy whatever as to right.

Parliament has a clear right, therefore, to interfere
on the prefent occafion; but, if it interferes without
providing an indemnity, it ufes its right in order to in-
flict a wrong, (its former fanction of the trade confidered.)

But the Britifh parliament will, perhaps, do more
than exercife a *general* right on this occafion. It may,

among

among other meafures, attempt to abolifh the flave-trade gradually, by impofing a tax upon negroes imported into the colonies, which tax fhall gradually increafe. This regulation, if it takes place, will evidently be one of a *commercial* nature, and certainly be much preferable to a forcible limitation of the number of negroes to be annually imported; inafmuch as it avoids all complication and partiality in the diftribution of the negroes fo imported, and furnifhes a fund of indemnity in each of the iflands, which, by the nature things, will bear a relative proportion to their refpective loffes. It will, indeed, by no means fully atone for thofe loffes, and therefore the mother-country muft add other funds; but, unlefs the minds of the colonifts fhall be previoufly poifoned, the law, in *this* particular, will ftand a chance of being popular in the iflands, and intereft a number of perfons in giving aid to its execution.

II. But while I fupport the authority of the mother-country in the above cafes, it is impoffible not to difcountenance a pretenfion, which there is, however, reafon to think is now abandoned by thofe who have hitherto maintained it; I mean, that of our having a right to controul *flavery in the iflands*. — An imperial power is given to Great Britain in matters of commerce, becaufe it is an united concern; but internal government is a concern which is confined within the limits
of

of the colonies. The degree of sovereignty, which the colonists enjoy within their own territories, is a matter as well of consent on our side as of right on theirs; for, whatever power this country might have thought itself intitled to on this subject, in the first instance, it has long since been abandoned, and settlements have been formed on the faith of a certain degree of independence. — After so clear a discrimination of authorities, therefore, whatever be the temptation to intermeddle, it would be highly imprudent to yield to it; and certainly not the wisest way of obtaining the ends of humanity, which are the objects of it. We may, therefore, safely assert, first, that we have no title to interpose as to any suppression or modification of slavery; secondly, that, if we attempt it, we shall excite a ferment among the slaves, already too much disposed to it; thirdly, that we shall chill the efforts of many moderate men in the colonies, who are disposed to plead in favour of this unhappy order of men, (lest advantage should be taken of their statements;) and, lastly, such attempts will be perfectly premature, mischevious, or useless, as the negroes are by no means ripe for emancipation, and as all provisions in their favour will depend for their execution on the concurrence and good-will of the colonists; not to mention that the very fear of a speedy abolition will, of itself, be the most powerful means of procuring a melioration of the lot of the slaves. If it be asked, when the period

L

riod of emancipation will arrive? I anfwer, as was anfwered in the Houfe of Commons, "that it cannot
" happen *for a generation to come,* becaufe the prefent
" generation of flaves is avowedly unfit for it."

III. The laft of the obfervations alluded to above,
which I fhall prefume to offer, is, like the two which
have preceded it, folely fuggefted with a view to tran-
quillity and mutual good-humour between the contending parties; and refpects the degree of oppofition
proper to be given to the progrefs of the flave-bill, now
pending in parliament. As this fubject is of the utmoft
importance, I fhall beg leave to attempt to diffuade the
colonifts from too obftinate a refiftance to their fate,
by the following arguments. — Firft, they can never
reverfe the vote of the Houfe of Commons, the progrefs of whofe fentiments on this fubject has been rapid
beyond belief. The general queftion about abolition, laft year, was *loft* by two to one, while the
queftion for a gradual abolition has now been *carried* by
three to one; and, merely upon a queftion of pro-
longing the flave-trade for a fingle year beyond the
term of three years, the colonies loft 30 friends,
which made a difference of 60 votes. If fuch
are the changes of temper in the Houfe, and if the
remains of attachment to the colonial fyftem, upon this
occafion, are proved to be thus flight; what have the
colonies to hope for by a farther refiftance? ———
In the next place, fuppofing they could alter the
vote,

vote, it would only *accumulate refentment* and irritate
their adverfaries to do their worft. It is impoffible
that parliamentary fpeaking can go for nothing. The
epifodes of Mr. Wuberforce, the fubtle arithmetic and
the glowing profpects and perorations of Mr. Pitt, the
vigorous fallies and farcafms or the pithy ftatements of
Mr. Fox, will again add to the number and dete ni-
nation of their enemies; and as the public originally
influenced the Houfe of Commons, fo the Houfe of
Commons by its late votes and debates will re-act and
and increafe the intereft of the public. In fhort, the
colonifts may now capitulate *on terms*; whereas next
year the enemy is likely to be fufficiently in force to
make them furrender at *difcretion.* — But who is there
that does not perceive that *popularity* is become need-
ful to the colonifts? The flave-trade is not their *only*
queftion: various others hang in a ftate of dangerous
fufpence. Individuals are feeking to precipitate minif-
ters into novelties and a fyftem of harfhnefs; and mi-
nifters feem to offer but a faint refiftance to them.
Individuals have even a formidable power, depending
folely on themfelves; namely, that of influencing the
confumption of colony-products both at home and a-
broad; affociations with perfons in foreign countries,
which are objects of hoftile proclamations in other inftances, being allowed in this inftance to have their full
force againft the colonifts and their moft important in-
terefts. — Another circumftance, no lefs alarming, is

the

the poffible *defection*, or *relaxation*, of their warmeſt
friends, of which many inſtances have already been given in the Houſe of Commons;* and the example
ſeems to have extended to ſome of the coloniſts; all of
whom, it muſt be obſerved, do not want negroes,
though all of them deſire to preſerve their charaĉters
and ſecure peace; and ſome of them (notwith-
ſtanding the opinion of Mr. Pitt) have been found not
incapable of modifying their ſyſtem, even in ſpite of
their intereſt.—Beſides, it is by no means wiſe to *for-
feit the pledge* of the great promoters of the abolition,
given in favour of a continuance of the trade for four
years longer, previous to its abolition; the power and
influence of theſe gentlemen being ſuch, as not to make
it prudent to value them lightly.—Have not the coloniſts, moreover, prayed for a deciſion; and, when it
is given, will it not ſeem unreaſonable not to ſubmit to
it, as well as unwiſe not to compound with it, leſt a
worſe thing ſhould happen? — Why too ſhould they be
too earneſt upon this occaſion, when they know, that,
if hard preſſed, they have a remedy in contraband;
which, though it may be checked by force, and, if

---

* Even Mr. Dundas's engagement to take the ſenſe of the Houſe
of Commons again, upon the ſlave queſtion, was only upon condition that the *regulations* to be enaĉted ſhould be ſuch as he could not
approve; but Mr. Pitt gave the Houſe reaſon to underſtand that they
would be ſuch as Mr. Dundas ſhould not only approve of, but him-
ſelf take a lead in propoſing.

moderation

moderation were ufed as to the abolition; would die fpontaneoufly; yet cannot be radically cured, if encouraged by ftrong temptations, without the zealous concurrence of various foreign powers.—But there is a reafon of another kind to be offered refpecting *humanity.* The trade has received its fentence of death in the opinion of the concerned; they have feen the hand-writing on the wall; and, having had warning to quit, like other tenants they wifh to rack the premifes. Africa will become the fubject of a fcramble: the black traders of that country will cry havock and let loofe the dogs of war. If the *fears* of the concerned are thoroughly awakened without any thing paffing in parliament, it is impoffible to check this mifchief, otherwife than by regulations; and, though the ceffation of the demand of flaves for St. Domingo, for fome time to come, will admit of an unufual quantity for the moment being fent to our iflands without any additional diftrefs to Africa; yet the confideration here urged will have fufficient weight even with the Lords, to lead them to pafs an early bill of regulation and reftraint, if not of abolition. — As to the Lords, their refiftance to the public impulfe may be ventured upon to a certain length; and the exertions of a certain great naval perfonage, who is in a fituation to feel the maritime refources, afforded by the Weft Indies, as a perfonal concern to himfelf, may greatly encourage them; but the times are too delicate for the Lords to ftand alone,

and

and rifk a junction of the affociations for abolifhing the flave-trade with the affociations formed for political purpofes.—There is another argument, of an interefted nature, which is by no means without its weight; for, if the colonifts yield with a good grace to what is propofed, and bend the great ftrength of their evidence to a ftatement of their neceffities and to the vindication of their characters, which, generally fpeaking, have been cruelly afperfed; their application for indemnity and relief will naturally fare the better. A vote in their favour will thus more readily be obtained from parliament, and the affent of the people will be more chearful in bearing the burthen impofed by that vote.

But, to proceed to the laft and ftrongeft confideration under this head. The colonifts will be utterly miftaken, if they think the oppofition they have to contend with is *tranfient*. The queftion will foon be delivered over in charge to the hands of thofe who are now young; and, there can be no doubt, that fchools and univerfities, that clergy and fectaries, and that authors and periodical writers of every defcription, are every where againft them; as well as the fofter fex, who, in the fituation of mothers, &c. will have a decifive influence over the rifing generation. Nor fhould it be forgotten, in a conteft of this fort, that time is daily carrying away perfons of the old political fchool, who were bred in the prejudices of their forefathers; and that fentiments are no longer heredi-

tary

tary in the prefent age, when men begin to think for themfelves, and feel a property in their opinions. — Befides, their is a popular principle to work upon, which never can abate in its force. The trade in quef- tion is a trade againft the perfons, the property, and the peace, of men, who have never harmed us. The trade has been arraigned and condemned, after every indulgence has been given it for a hearing; but, alas! no juftification, or even extenuation, could be offered at that hearing: only arguments of policy, which are now but faintly attended to, and certain objections as to practicability; and even a Weft-India meeting, at the London-Tavern, has generoufly avowed, that they have no wifh to oppofe the civilization of Africa, and only defire to fhare in the trade for flaves, while it is left open to others. — But the caufe is not only popular, but it is one, of all others, liable to be *kept in agitation*. Men love to be righteous at the ex- pence of other people, and acting upon each other is held equivalent to acting for themfelves. In fhort, vicarious merit, and virtue by fubftitution, form a fort of *commutation*-fyftem, by which men eafily con- tent themfelves refpecting their own conduct. Virtue muft, in general, confift in *effort*, fince it would not be worth while making a point with mankind of what is commonly fpontaneous; while *criticifm*, on the other hand, is *eafy and pleafant*, being, perhaps, an irritative paffion implanted in us, in order to operate as a cor-
rective

rective towards others for the improvement of the race at large. It is becaufe religious perfecution has been founded upon thefe active and permanent principles, that it has been furious as well as univerfal, fo as unhappily, not, even to this moment, to be extinguifhed in our own nation.

The colonifts, therefore, would do wifely to make up their minds to their fate at once; particularly fince, if this bill paffes, the legal trade in flaves is gone *for ever*, as the Houfe of Commons will always oppofe a negative upon its reftoration. Something, however, has been faved from fhipwreck in the conteft : calumnies on the colonifts have been fomewhat difcredited ; the poffibility of obtaining white men to labour in tropical countries is given up; the flavery actually fubfifting in the iflands feems allowed to remain untouched ; and the negroes are agreed to be unfit for prefent emancipation. In fhort, the abolition of flavery itfelf in the iflands is left to its own fate ; and, as the children of the Weft Indians, wherever fent out of the iflands for education, will be made afhamed, if not averfe, with refpect to the poffeffion of flaves ; one of two things will happen; either flavery will become fo mild, as only to be fuch in name ; or it will be formally abolifhed, as heretofore in Europe, by the decifion of thofe who are interefted in it ; and thus fuffer what Mr. Hume would call an *Euthanafia.*

To

To conclude, every day has prefented various afpects refpecting the fate of the flave-trade. No man could tell, on the fide of the coloniits, what ought to be his own conduct, till he faw the conduct of others. But the thing at la t has taken a fixed fhape, and the colonifts have no courfe left but that of moderation. Their late petition to the Lords, though it has contributed its *fhare* to poftpone the great decifion for a feffion, will eafily be forgiven, as an act of juftice to abfent friends, and as forming a bafis for their own indemnity ; though it is to be obferved, that it is not a meafure in which all the colonifts have been engaged. — Let the colonifts be wife only in what remains. *What can't be cured muft be endured !*

If the colonifts anfwer to this advice ; " We have " friends at *court*, and fhall furrender nothing which " we can keep;" I reply, that, if perfons have friends, it is ftill a queftion of moment, when and how to ufe them ; and the queftion is for *their* confideration rather than that of others. In the decifion of it, the arguments I have ufed merit fome attention. — I fhall only add, that, if the fupport of thefe friends can be directed to other points which have been agitated above, it will be a proof of their friendfhip greatly wanted.—But, *in any event*, the colonifts muft allow that no affurances and no profpects can juftify their not providing refources in cafe of a defeat. The purchafe of negroes, particularly females, will be purfued with avidity, and does

not

not require alluding to; except to check the ardour of the colonifts, who will be apt, in fome cafes, to pur-chafe more negroes at a time, than can eafily be taken care of in a domeftic view, or than will be fafe in a pub-lic one. What I would rather notice regards the mea-fures requifite to increafe births, leffen deaths, procure fubftitutes for negro labour, introduce morality and Chriftianity among the negroes, and bind their attach-ment; and, at the fame time, to fupprefs the cruelties of individuals towards them.—On thefe fubjects, a multi-tude of hints might here be offered, but they will be referved for a future occafion.

THE END.

*9 7 8 3 3 3 7 3 0 6 7 5 5 *